ANCIENT TECHNOLOGY

ANCIENT
TRANSPORTATION

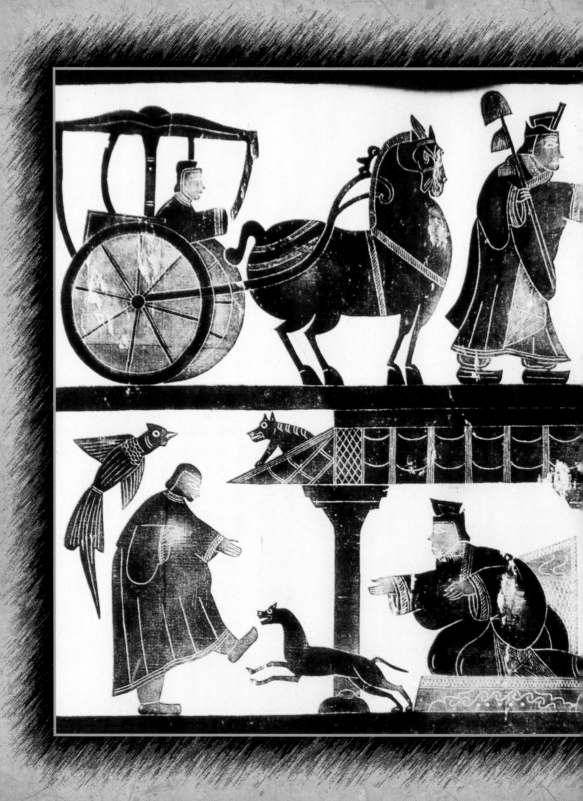

ANCIENT TECHNOLOGY

ANCIENT TRANSPORTATION

FROM CAMELS TO CANALS

by Michael Woods
and
Mary B. Woods

RP RUNESTONE PRESS • MINNEAPOLIS
AN IMPRINT OF LERNER PUBLISHING GROUP

Dedicated to John and Catherine Woods, Joseph and Mary Boyle

Series designer: Zachary Marell
Series editors: Joelle E. Riley and Dina Drits
Copy editor: Margaret J. Goldstein
Photograph researcher: Dan Mahoney

Runestone Press
An imprint of Lerner Publishing Group
241 First Avenue North
Minneapolis, MN 55401 U.S.A.

Website address: www.lernerbooks.com

Library of Congress Cataloging-in-Publication Data

Woods, Michael, 1946–
    Ancient transportation : from camels to canals / by Michael Woods and Mary B. Woods.
       p. cm. — (Ancient technology)
    Includes bibliographical references and index.
    Summary: Surveys transportation technology in various cultures from the Stone Age to A.D. 476, including China, Egypt, Mesoamerica, and Greece.
    ISBN 0-8225-2993-9 (lib. bdg. : alk. paper)
    1. Transportation—History—Juvenile literature.
[1. Transportation—History.] I. Woods, Mary B.
(Mary Boyle), 1946– . II. Title. III. Series.
TA1149.W66 2000
629.04'09'01—dc21   98-47475

Manufactured in the United States of America
3 4 5 6 7 8 – JR – 07 06 05 04 03 02

TABLE OF CONTENTS

What do you think of when you hear the word *technology*? You probably think of something totally new. You might think of research laboratories filled with computers, powerful microscopes, and other scientific tools. But technology doesn't refer to just brand-new machines and discoveries. Technology is as old as human society.

Technology is the use of knowledge, inventions, and discoveries to make life better. The word *technology* comes from two Greek words. One, *techne*, means "art" or "craft." The other, *logos*, means "logic" or "reason." Ancient Greeks originally used the word *technology* to mean a discussion of arts and crafts. But in modern times, *technology* usually refers to the craft, technique, or tool itself.

There are many kinds of technology. Medicine is one kind. Agriculture and machinery are others. This book looks at yet another kind of technology—one that has been improving human society for millions of years. That is the technology of transportation.

Transportation, the movement of people and goods, has always had great importance in human life. People need methods of transportation to escape enemies, move goods to market, communicate, and reach new and better living places. When we think of transportation, we often think of vehicles such as ships and wagons. But transportation technology includes more than just vehicles.

Maps, ports, lighthouses, bridges, and methods for delivering and handling shipments are all part of transportation technology.

Ancient Roots

You've probably heard people remark, "There's nothing new under the sun!" That's often true when we're talking about transportation. Modern engineers and scientists rarely make advances in transportation technology that are totally new. Engineers might figure out how to make roads last longer, wheels turn faster, or bridges span greater distances. But often these accomplishments are just improvements on ideas and techniques developed in earlier times. For example, modern superhighways, with their sides that slope downward from the center, are based on an ancient Roman design.

Historians use the word *ancient* to describe the period from the emergence of the first humans on earth to the fall of the Western Roman Empire in A.D. 476. The first human beings lived about 2.5 million years ago. The use of technology is one of many traits that historians use to distinguish humans from their prehuman ancestors.

Technology's Spread

The Phoenicians were the master shipbuilders of the ancient world. With their well-made ships, Phoenician sailors were able to cross the Mediterranean Sea from the

CIVILIZATIONS OF THE
Ancient World
(through A.D. 476)

EUROPE

ASIA

AFRICA

Indian
Ocean

6000 B.C. ━━━━━━━━━ 534 B.C.		Middle East
3100 B.C. ━━━━━━━━ 30 B.C.		Egypt
1766 B.C. ━━━━━━━━━		China
1200 B.C. ━━━━━━━━━		Mesoamerica
800 B.C. ━━━━ 146 B.C.		Greece
509 B.C. ━━━━ A.D. 476		Rome
320 B.C. ━━━━		India

Stone Age civilizations have flourished in
most parts of the world. These cultures began and
ended at different times in different regions.

Middle East and go beyond it. They established colonies in other countries and even sailed into the Atlantic Ocean as far as England. They traded a costly purple dye and fine cedar logs for gold, copper, ivory, and other products. Through trade, the Phoenicians spread knowledge and ideas. Historians call them "carriers of civilization."

They were also carriers of technology. The ancient Greeks adopted a lot of Phoenician shipbuilding technology. The Greeks traded with the Romans, so Roman ships inevitably resembled Greek vessels, which resembled Phoenician vessels. Although each group added improvements, the basic Mediterranean ship in the ancient world was based on Phoenician technology.

Ancient people left us a rich legacy of transportation technology. This book tells the story of this technology and how it improved ancient life. Read on and discover many amazing techniques that helped move the ancient world— and continue to help move the modern world.

THE STONE AGE

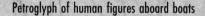
Petroglyph of human figures aboard boats

The first humans lived on earth about 2.5 million years ago. These Stone Age people were hunters and gatherers. They survived by fishing, catching game, gathering wild plants, hunting woolly mammoths and other animals, and eating the remains of kills left by predatory animals.

Stone Age people were almost constantly traveling. When the food supply in one region became exhausted, people moved to another place with a more abundant supply. They followed migrating herds of animals that supplied meat, furs, bones, and other materials. Natural disasters such as droughts, wildfires, volcanic eruptions, and climate changes also forced Stone Age people to move.

Speed was often important. Hunters who slew an elk had to bring it back to the safety of their camp before animals stole it. Sometimes Stone Age people had to move quickly to escape enemies. Transportation in the Stone Age was a matter of life and death.

Stone Age people probably had few possessions. But they must have traveled with blankets, stone and bone tools, and other heavy objects. People with the fastest and most efficient ways of carrying the heaviest loads, while moving from one place to another had the best chance to survive.

THE FIRST BRIDGES

When they were on the move, Stone Age hunters and gatherers needed convenient ways to cross natural barriers such as rivers and ravines. The first bridges formed naturally. Lightning strikes, wind, and soil erosion often sent trees crashing to the ground. Occasionally, a tree fell in just the right position to allow people to climb across a river.

The first bridge builder was the first person to deliberately fell a tree or position a log to span a narrow stream. People then realized they could cross even wider streams by placing tree trunks end to end, supported by a rock in midstream. The rock was the first support pier. Stone Age people may also have built bridges out of large flat stones placed across a stream—or from vines strung from one side to the other.

THE FIRST BOATS

Stone Age people surely noticed tree trunks floating down rivers. After floods, people probably saw birds, raccoons, and other animals clinging to floating logs. These people saw how rapidly and effortlessly the animals traveled downstream. Eventually, people also clung to logs, kicking with their feet, and paddling with their hands. Others grabbed floating objects to keep from drowning. These simple floats were the first boats.

Next, Stone Age people began to lash logs together to make rafts, which were more stable than individual logs and could carry heavier loads. Archaeologists, scientists who study the remains of past cultures, believe that Stone Age people made the first dugout canoes, using tools to hollow out logs. Dugout canoes are still used in some parts of the world.

Australian Aborigines used simple bark boats, even into the early twentieth century. The Aborigines would cut a big strip of bark from a tree and seal the ends of the strip with clay. Archaeologists think that Stone Age people made the same kind of bark boat.

Modern-day dugout canoe from Saint Lucia, a Caribbean island nation

Archaeologists have found strong evidence that the first long-distance sea voyages occurred in the Stone Age. In Japan, they have discovered stone tools that are a hundred thousand years old. How did early humans get to Japan, an island group in the Pacific Ocean? They must have traveled by boat from Korea, a hundred miles across the ocean, probably stopping at numerous islands along the way.

Archaeologists have also discovered 50,000 stone tools in the desert of central Australia. Australia is surrounded by water. How did Stone Age people reach the continent? They must have floated thousands of miles across the Indian Ocean, with many island stops en route, to get there.

A Sweet Road

The very first roads were paths of packed earth. Some roads were made by animals—trampled down as deer, elk, and other creatures repeatedly took the same route to watering spots. Stone Age people made roads in the same way—with their own feet.

In A.D. 1970, a man named Raymond Sweet discovered the remains of a six-thousand-year-old elevated wooden walkway preserved in a bog in southwestern England. Archaeologists think it was the first road that was actually built, rather than trampled. The road became known as the Sweet Track.

The Sweet Track consisted of tree branches hammered into soft soil in an **X** pattern. The upper arms of the **X**s extended above ground level. Using stone tools, builders split planks from tree trunks and laid the planks in the crotches of the **X**s. People then walked along a pathway formed by the overlapping planks.

The road apparently allowed people to walk through a low, swampy area and may have connected nearby settlements. Why did Stone Age people settle in a swampy area? The swamp would have been an abundant source of food and building material. It probably supplied fish, deer, wild pigs, and other animals, as well as reeds for thatching huts.

YOKE, TRAVOIS (SLIDE CAR)

Stone Age hunters probably dreaded the work of transporting a dead animal back to camp. It must have been an ordeal just to get a grip on the carcass. Archaeologists believe that early hunters used a simple device called a yoke to help them carry awkward loads.

A yoke was a branch cut from a tree. A Stone Age hunter probably fastened small game to one end of the branch and carried the other end over his shoulder. A double yoke was a pole balanced over a person's shoulders with loads fastened on each end. Two hunters also could tie a large carcass onto a yoke, with each hunter carrying one end.

The yoke led to the development of a vehicle called a travois (also called a slide car). The first travois probably was a forked tree branch with a load on the forked portion. The other end of the branch was pulled by hand, or perhaps fastened to someone's waist. The loaded end simply dragged along the ground. Even the most primitive travois enabled people to carry heavy loads farther than ever before.

Later, travois were pulled by beasts of burden—work animals. Native Americans used a travois consisting of two long poles, connected with crossbars or a platform, and harnessed to a horse.

Stone Age Sneakers

The human foot is, of course, the oldest means of transportation. Improvements in foot travel usually involve improvements in footwear. Look at modern sneakers. They are made with advanced adhesives and high-tech fabrics. Chambers of nitrogen gas, minipumps, and tiny valves help cushion the foot and give added spring to the step.

The first foot coverings were much more basic but nonetheless a great technological advance over bare feet. Shoes and sandals enabled people to travel farther, in colder weather, over rougher terrain, all while carrying heavier loads.

Archaeologists believe that Stone Age people in cold regions of Asia and Europe made the first foot coverings. These probably were animal skins that helped protect against cold and snow. People quickly realized that the skins also protected their feet from injury and made travel more comfortable.

Ancient people later developed warm-weather footgear from a variety of materials. Egyptian wall paintings show people wearing sandals with soles made from papyrus. Clogs probably began in ancient Japan. They were carved wooden soles fastened to the feet with vines or ropes. In the ancient Middle East, shoemakers added thick soles for rough terrain, laces to keep shoes securely fastened, and heel guards to protect feet from injury. Men in ancient Greece wore tough leather boots in battle and while hunting. Women and girls sometimes wore fashionable ankle-height boots.

The concept of wearing different shoes for different purposes caught on in ancient Rome. People there wore light sandals called *solea,* ankle-height leather shoes called *calcei,* and a variety of other styles. For long marches, Roman soldiers wore *caligae*—heavy, high-topped boots with hobnailed (studded with short, large-headed nails) soles. The boots had open toes for ventilation and rapid drying after marches in wet weather.

For many centuries, however, most of the world went barefoot. Like a lot of new technology, shoes were expensive in ancient times and available only to the rich and to the military.

Egyptian leather sandals
made over five thousand years ago

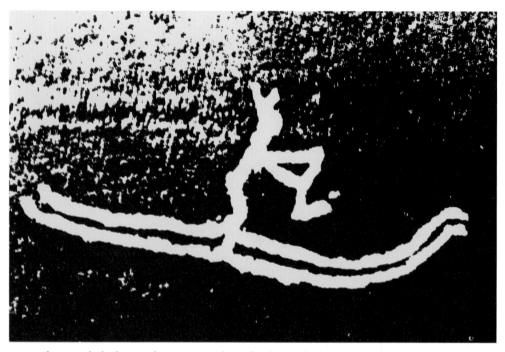

This petroglyph, discovered in Norway, is the earliest known depiction of a skier.

SKIS AND SLEDGES

Archaeologists have long assumed that Stone Age people used skis for winter travel in cold areas of Asia and Europe. Wood was abundant in these areas, and it took no great ingenuity to realize that a long flat board could glide easily over snow. But wood rots quickly, and for a long time archaeologists had no physical evidence that early humans used skis.

But, in A.D. 1964, Russian archaeologists discovered the remains of a ski preserved in the acid soil of a peat bog in northeastern Russia. Laboratory analysis of the wood indicated that the ski was made around 6000 B.C.

In another finding, a 4,500-year-old Norwegian rock carving depicts a skier using a single pole for propulsion and skis that were probably 10 feet long. Early ski makers probably recognized that long skis improve stability. The skier even showed proper form—leaning forward slightly, with knees bent.

Stone Age people probably did not ski for recreation, as many modern people do. Rather, hunters probably used skis to find game and to carry kills back to their families. Warriors may also have used skis in winter battles.

Drawings made in ancient Mesopotamia around 3500 B.C. show sledges, which are like sleighs. The first sledges probably were just flat boards used to drag things over land. The addition of skilike runners created a vehicle ideal for pulling heavy loads over snow and ice.

BEASTS OF BURDEN

The Old Stone Age, or Paleolithic period, lasted until about 10,000 B.C. During the New Stone Age, or Neolithic period, which lasted until about 3500 B.C., people began to abandon the hunter-gatherer lifestyle and become more settled. They formed permanent villages and farms. They grew grain, vegetables, and fruit. They domesticated wild animals.

Scientists have discovered the remains of domesticated dogs that lived 10,000 years ago. Scientists believe that dogs were the first beasts of burden. Dogs might have been used to pull vehicles such as slide cars. People later harnessed larger animals to vehicles. With these draft animals (*draft* means "pull"), people could move enormous loads over great distances.

Scientists regard the ass as the world's first draft animal.

Asses, which are related to horses, once lived wild in the Mediterranean area. They are slower than horses but, when domesticated, are more docile and surefooted. Early traders used asses as pack animals—cargo was loaded on their backs. After the invention of the wheel, warriors used asses to pull chariots. Ancient people used a variety of other draft animals, including oxen, buffalo, reindeer, elephants, yaks, llamas, and camels.

There are two kinds of camel. The dromedary, or Arabian camel, has one hump. The Bactrian camel has two. Both camels have been domesticated since ancient times. Their humps store nutrients that allow the camels to live for long periods without water or food. Dromedaries have thick, wide hooves that help them move across hot desert sand. These camels can even seal their nostrils to avoid inhaling dust. The Bactrian camel is more suited to rocky, cooler regions.

Camels were an excellent means of transportation in ancient times. Riding dromedaries, people could cover more than a hundred miles per day. A Bactrian camel could carry up to a thousand pounds of cargo and cover up to 30 miles per day. Camels also supplied travelers with milk, meat, and cloth. They shed their long hair every summer, and people wove it into fabric.

Use of the camel was a great advance in the history of land transportation. Camels allowed people to establish regular contact with other groups and to establish trade routes across vast deserts.

2

ANCIENT MIDDLE EAST

The word *civilization* comes from the Latin *civitas*, meaning "city." Historians use the word to refer to settled societies with systems of government, religion, social class, labor, and record keeping.

Around 6000 B.C., civilizations began to develop in the ancient Middle East, or Near East—the region where Asia, Africa, and Europe meet. This region contains the Fertile Crescent, an arc of fertile land extending from the eastern Mediterranean Sea to the Persian Gulf. Because the land was good for farming, people settled there in permanent villages. Some people settled between the Tigris and Euphrates Rivers in what is present-day Iraq. The Greeks later named the region Mesopotamia, which means "between rivers."

The first great civilization in Mesopotamia was Sumer. The Sumerians invented the wheel, a system of writing called cuneiform, and other technologies. Other groups in Mesopotamia included the Babylonians and the Assyrians.

The Phoenicians developed a civilization on the eastern shore of the Mediterranean Sea in modern-day Syria and Lebanon. They built great port cities such as Sidon and Tyre and established distant trading posts, including the famous city of Carthage in North Africa.

Geography and natural resources often influence transportation technology. With the Tigris and Euphrates Rivers and the Mediterranean Sea nearby, Middle Eastern people naturally turned to the water for transportation.

RAFTS, FLOATS, AND RIVERBOATS

Around 2000 B.C., the Assyrians built boats called *keleks*, the forerunners of modern inflatable rafts. Keleks were made from many individual sheepskins, sewed up to form airtight bags that were inflated like balloons. The inflated skins were fastened under a frame of strong willow rods, topped by a platform covered with reeds or moss. Some big keleks contained 20 inflated sheepskins. Keleks floated close to the surface. Like modern rafts, they were able to bounce off rocks and zoom through white water without damage. They were ideal for carrying passengers and freight safely through rapids in mountain streams.

The Assyrians also used inflated sheepskins as individual floats—much the same way modern children use inner tubes and water wings. Ancient pictures show people floating in the water on inflated skins. They probably used the floats more for work than play. It took a great deal of time and effort to prepare a sheepskin with airtight seams. The floats probably were far too expensive for use as toys. The pictures show men floating alongside keleks and apparently helping to steer the rafts.

The Assyrians used sheepskins to make yet another kind of boat—a circular riverboat for transporting freight, soldiers, and civilians. The skins were stretched over a framework of willow rods or reeds. Seams were sealed with pitch to prevent leaks. Some of the boats were small, suitable for just one or two people. Others could carry heavy cargo. Ancient writers said that the biggest boats could carry five "talents," which added up to somewhere near 290 pounds.

Herodotus, a Greek historian who lived from 484 to 425 B.C., marveled at these riverboats during a visit to the Middle East. He wrote:

> Two men standing upright steer the boat, each with a paddle, one drawing it to him, the other thrusting it from him. There is a live ass in each boat, or more than one in the larger. So when they have floated down to Babylon and disposed of their cargo, they sell the framework of the boat and all the reeds. The hides are set on the backs of asses, which are then driven back to Armenia, for it is not by any means possible to go up the stream by water, by reason of the swiftness of the current. It is for this reason that they make their boats of hides and not wood. When they have driven their asses back to Armenia, they make more boats in the same way.

THE SAIL

The earliest ancient boats were powered by people using oars and paddles. The first people to realize the advantages of wind power over rowers were probably the Phoenicians. They introduced sails on their *gauli*, round ships used for long sea voyages around 3000 B.C. Sails were made of heavy fabric such as linen.

Seventh century B.C. Middle Eastern plan of the world on a clay tablet. Mesopotamia is surrounded by a ring, which represents the ocean. Beyond this ocean lies chaos.

The First Maps

Where is it? How do I get there? What is the fastest and easiest route? People have asked such questions for thousands of years.

Stone Age people probably made the first maps by scratching in the soil with sticks. Perhaps they drew the location of rivers, lakes, mountains, and herds of game. Archaeologists suspect that some of the cave paintings and etchings that have been found on animal tusks may be early maps. Some of these pictures date to the Old Stone Age. But experts aren't sure whether these pictures are true maps or just decorative illustrations.

The first true maps were made on clay tablets in Mesopotamia. They date to around 2300 B.C. The tablets have all the essential characteristics of maps: diagrams of land features and clearly visible markers for the cardinal points—north, south, east, and west. Many early Mesopotamian maps appear to be legal records of land purchases. These maps mark off the exact dimensions of lots and fields. Other maps were clearly used to help transport people and goods over long distances.

One ancient Babylonian map, possibly the earliest world map, shows the earth as it was known to the Babylonians around 500 B.C. The map shows the world as a disk, with the Persian Gulf, Babylon, and other Middle Eastern countries in the center. The mapmaker showed an immense ocean surrounding these countries, and beyond the ocean were four "remote regions" believed to be at the very edge of the world. One of the regions was a mysterious land where "the sun is not seen." Where do you think it might have been?

The word *gauli* comes from a Phoenician term meaning "milk pail," which gauli resembled. The design may have looked awkward, but the ships carried more cargo than any previous boat. Gauli were the first freighters. They were also used as warships.

Gauli relied on a single large sail, a design that prevailed for about three thousand years. The sail was fixed in one position. It could not be raised or lowered in response to changing wind conditions like a modern sail. A sailor could not "beat against the wind"—or manipulate the sail to take advantage of otherwise unfavorable conditions. Vessels could make progress only when the wind blew in the right direction. Thus, ancient sea transport was often disrupted by unfavorable winds and storms.

Gauli also had oars, which were used mainly for entering and clearing harbors. In wartime, captains relied on the sail as much as possible, to conserve the strength of the rowers for battle. But just before battle, the sail and mast were removed and left on a nearby beach. There was good reason for this practice. Ancient warships often rammed each other, and a collision could knock the mast off one or both of the vessels.

HORSE POWER

Stone Age cave paintings and carvings on animal tusks show that humans have known about horses for more than 30,000 years. Cave paintings often show people hunting horses. Stone Age people probably regarded the animals as just a tasty meal on hooves.

Sometime between 4000 B.C. and 3000 B.C., people in the ancient Middle East tamed wild horses. They captured

Assyrian relief from around 700 B.C. of Phoenician ships carrying timber

them, fed them, and tended to their illnesses and injuries. A small clay figurine found north of modern-day Damascus, Syria, depicts a domestic horse. The figurine dates to about 2300 B.C.

At first, people probably kept horses for meat, milk, and goods that could be made from horsehair and hide. Later, people used them to carry packs on trade routes. After the wheel was invented, horses pulled carts, wagons, and chariots.

Some experts think that ancient people kept horses mainly to breed mules. A mule is the offspring of a female horse and a male donkey. Mules look a lot like horses but have larger ears, smaller hooves, and a tufted tail. They are more surefooted and are hardier than horses.

SADDLE UP!

Riding on horseback became popular after 2000 B.C. But early horses were not very large—probably not more than 12 hands in height at the shoulder. (The width of a human hand—about four inches—is the standard measure of horse height.) The rump was the highest part of a horse's back. A rider had to sit on the horse's rump or his feet would drag on the ground. Before horseback riding could become really practical, horses had to be bred for greater size.

Early riders controlled their mounts with a whip in one hand and a rein from a nose ring in the other. Mouth bits, bridles, and other control technology came between 4000 B.C. and 3000 B.C., from tribes who occupied what now is southern Russia and Eastern Europe. Saddles evolved from simple blankets that riders used to protect themselves from horsehair scratches.

Eventually, horses became essential in warfare. Horses were used to pull war chariots, and a soldier's life often depended on the stamina and training of his horse. Around 1350 B.C., a master horseman named Kikkuli wrote the first systematic plan for the care and feeding of the chariot horse. Here is part of Kikkuli's recipe for a strong and healthy horse:

Day 2—Pace one league [three miles], run one furlong [one-eighth mile]. Feed two handsful grass, one of clover, four handsful barley. Graze all night.

Day 4—Pace two leagues in morning, one at night. No water all day. Grass at night.

Day 5—Pace two leagues, run 20 furlongs out and 30 furlongs home. Put rugs on. After sweating, give one pail of salted water and one pail of malt-water. Take to river and wash down. Swim horses. Take to stable and give further pail of malted water and pail of salted water. Wash and swim again. Feed at night one bushel boiled barley with chaff.

Day 11—Anoint all over with butter.

Why butter? Ancient people sometimes massaged their sore muscles and joints with butter. They probably regarded it as a tonic for horses as well.

AROUND COMES THE WHEEL

No other technology can match the wheel in its simplicity and impact on society. With wheels, vehicles can move quickly and efficiently. Wheels are also the building blocks of gears, pulleys, and other machines. By using animals to pull wheeled vehicles, ancient people saw improvements in farming, trade, and other areas.

The oldest known picture of a wheel appears on a clay tablet dating from about 3500 B.C. It was found in Uruk, an ancient Sumerian city. The picture shows a sledge with two small disks attached. (It is actually a four-wheeled vehicle shown in profile.) Archaeologists have found remains of actual wheeled vehicles used around 2700 B.C.

Contrary to popular belief, people did not invent the wheel for transportation. Nor did wheels evolve from the practice of using logs as rollers placed under heavy objects.

World's oldest known wooden wheel, made 5,200 years ago

Indeed, some experts believe ancient people never used log rollers.

Instead, archaeologists think the first wheels were potter's wheels—wooden disks spun in a horizontal position, used to shape lumps of clay into vessels. How did a potter's wheel become a cart wheel? Perhaps carpenters moved newly completed potter's wheels by rolling them. Perhaps children rolled the wheels as toys and some creative adult—or child—attached them to an axle (a rod in the center of a wheel around which the wheel turns) made of sticks and put a sledge on top. Do you have other ideas?

Experts believe that the wheel was invented only once,

in Mesopotamia, and quickly spread to other civilizations. There is evidence of wheel use in India and China just after 3500 B.C., and in Egypt by 2500 B.C.

Other civilizations tried the wheel and found it unsuitable. People in some parts of the Far East and Middle East, for instance, preferred camels to wheeled carts. Camels were more efficient for travel over desert sands and rough terrain.

BETTER WHEELS AND AXLES

At first, wheel making was probably a simple matter that involved cutting a slab of wood from a round tree trunk. People later realized that sturdier wheels could be made from separate pieces of wood, positioned so the grain would not fray from contact with a road. For a thousand years after their invention, wheels were made from three thick pieces of wood, held together by strips of wood fastened to the side.

People eventually learned how to reduce the weight of the tripartite (three-part) wheel by carving out inner sections of the disk. The spoke wheel was invented in Mesopotamia around 2000 B.C. It was much lighter than a solid wheel and moved faster.

By 1400 B.C., Egyptian woodworkers were making strong, light wheels by putting together separate rims, spokes, and hubs. The parts were joined, carefully shaved, and adjusted for proper balance. These improved wheels were first used on expensive racing and war chariots, and by wealthy people who drove ancient versions of sports cars. The first tires were strips of copper or bronze nailed to the outside of wheels to reduce wear.

An axle that connected wheel to vehicle was essential. The first axles were strong wooden poles that sometimes extended through a central hole in the wheel. A peg through the axle kept the wheel attached. Some axles were fixed to, and turned with, wheels. Other axles allowed wheels to roll independently.

ANCIENT EGYPT

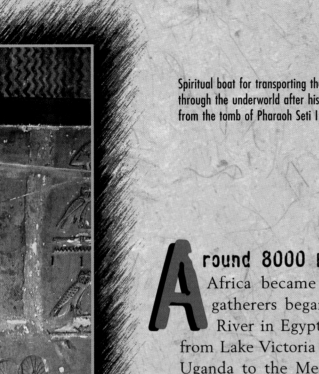

Around 8000 B.C., the climate in North Africa became drier, and ancient hunter-gatherers began to move toward the Nile River in Egypt. Flowing north 4,145 miles from Lake Victoria in modern-day Tanzania and Uganda to the Mediterranean Sea, the Nile is the longest river in the world.

By about 7000 B.C., people had built permanent settlements along the river. The Nile flooded its banks every July, soaking the soil and depositing fertile, mudlike silt on the surrounding land. Here early Egyptian farmers grew an abundance of wheat, barley, vegetables, and fruits.

The Nile was a natural highway for transporting goods and people. Traders in reed ships floated with the current and deposited their cargoes at Thebes, Memphis, and Giza. Then they sailed against the current back to home ports. From the mouth of the Nile, Egyptian merchants established trading routes that led to Asia, Greece, and other places.

NAVIGATING THE NILE

The first Egyptian boats were rafts made from tightly woven papyrus reeds. Boaters used poles to guide the rafts through shallow water. A wall painting completed around 3500 B.C. shows papyrus boats with crews of rowers. One of the crew members uses a steering paddle to guide the boat.

Eventually, the Egyptians attached a mast and square sail to their boats. The sail was not fixed permanently in the open position, as it was on Phoenician ships. Instead, the sail could be raised or lowered for use only when needed. Ships traveling south on the Nile, against the current, needed a sail. Luckily for the sailors, prevailing winds in Egypt are from the north. When traveling north, sailors lowered the sail and ran with the current. The ships also had oars for power in calm weather and for maneuvering near docks.

Passengers, crew, and cargo rode on deck under cloth awnings. Some Egyptian ships had cabins for passengers, with shades that rolled up and down.

SEAFARING VESSELS

The Egyptians built larger boats to ply trade routes on the Mediterranean Sea. Some of these vessels were 180 feet long and 60 feet wide. Archaeologists found the remains of one magnificent ship buried in sand near the Great Pyramid at Giza. (The Great Pyramid is the tomb of Pharaoh Khufu, who lived around 2600 B.C., and is one of the Seven Wonders of the Ancient World. The Wonders are a listing of the world's most notable objects built between about 3000 B.C. and A.D. 476, drawn up by ancient Greeks and Romans.) The 120-foot ship was actually a ceremonial barge, meant to assist Khufu on his journey to the afterlife.

Archaeologists have found other model boats in tombs. They are equipped with canopies, sails, and model rowers— even a sailor using a plumb line to check the water's depth.

Five-thousand-year-old funeral boat reassembled from well-preserved segments found near the tomb of Pharaoh Khufu

Three-thousand-year-old Egyptian papyrus showing workers dragging building blocks

SLEDGES BUILT THE PYRAMIDS

Sledges can slide over ice, snow, marshy ground, and even sand. They may seem simple. But sledges actually represent a milestone in people's ability to transport heavy loads.

Archaeologists believe sledges played a big role in moving the extremely heavy blocks of stone (some weighed more than four thousand pounds) used to build Egypt's pyramids, obelisks, statues, and other famous monuments. Sledges pulled by gangs of men were used to transport stones from rock quarries to the Nile and onto barges, and from the barges to building sites. Sledges were also used to move the blocks up temporary earthen ramps and into position at building sites.

THE FIRST PAVED ROADS

People seldom develop new technology unless a need exists. And sometimes one form of technology creates the need for another. Archaeologists believe that such a link exists between sledges and paved roads. The Egyptians used sledges to carry heavy blocks of stone across desert sands. But extremely heavy loads made the sledges immovable. They simply sank into the sand. So the Egyptians decided to pave the sand.

The remains of one paved road extend about 7.5 miles through the desert southwest of Cairo. Discovered by the U.S. Geological Survey in A.D. 1994, it is thought to be the oldest paved road in the world. Artifacts found along the road indicate that it was used between 2600 B.C. and 2134 B.C. It has an average width of 6.5 feet and is made from slabs of sandstone and limestone laid end to end.

Ancient Egyptians built the road to haul stones on sledges from a rock quarry to a dock at ancient Lake Moeris, in northern Egypt, near the Nile River. A channel connected the lake to the Nile. At the dock of the lake, the stones were loaded onto barges and floated down the channel to the Nile. The stones were then floated downriver to pyramid sites.

THE ANCIENT SUEZ CANAL

This famous Egyptian waterway gives ships a shortcut from the Mediterranean Sea to the Red Sea. Without this 101-mile-long channel, freighters, oil tankers, passenger ships, and warships traveling east from Europe would have to sail around the tip of Africa to reach ports in the Indian Ocean. The canal reduces transportation times between Europe and the Far East by weeks and reduces distances by thousands of miles.

Many historians trace the canal's origins to A.D. 1854 and a French diplomat named Ferdinand-Marie de Lesseps. De Lesseps enlisted the Egyptian government in the canal construction project, which lasted from A.D. 1859 to 1869.

Your history textbook may have been wrong about the Suez Canal. The first Suez Canal was built more than three thousand years earlier. In the thirteenth century B.C., ancient Egyptian engineers dug a canal that also allowed ships to pass directly from the Mediterranean Sea to the Red Sea. It followed a different route, linking a branch of the Nile River, just north of Cairo, with the Red Sea. Historians believe the project originated with Seti I, a pharaoh who reigned from about 1303 to 1290 B.C., or Ramses II, who ruled from 1290 to 1224 B.C.

We know the canal existed, partly because of murals inside a great temple near Thebes. The temple was built by Queen Hatshepsut, an Egyptian pharaoh who ruled from 1503 to 1482 B.C. Hatshepsut was the first female ruler known to history. The murals tell how Hatshepsut and a fleet of ships sailed the canal to the mysterious land of Punt, in eastern Africa. The voyage opened up trade between Egypt and other parts of Africa. For years after the trip, Egypt exported gold, incense, ebony, myrrh, fruit, and other products through the canal to Punt.

The first Suez Canal gradually lost its importance. It was filled in by blowing sand and forgotten. Then King Darius I

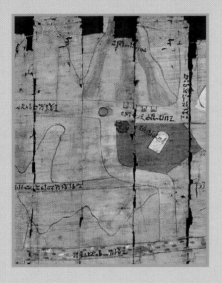

Turin Papyrus, a map depicting the route to gold mines in the Sinai Peninsula, Egypt

The Treasure Map

Ancient Egyptians carved maps in stone, drew maps on papyrus scrolls, and painted maps on pottery and tomb walls. With a single known exception, however, these were not true maps intended to help people find their way from one location to another. Rather, the maps were religious and symbolic documents. Some, for instance, showed secret routes to the afterlife. Others presented astronomers' concepts of the universe.

Archaeologists have found one true ancient Egyptian map in the Turin Papyrus, a document written around 1200 B.C. The map shows the route to gold mines in a mountainous region of Egypt along the Red Sea. The map is even color coded. A key indicates that gold-bearing mountains are shown in red.

of Persia, who lived from 550 to 486 B.C. and also ruled Egypt, got a brilliant idea. Darius wrote:

> I commanded a canal be dug from the river Nile to the Sea which goes from Persia. This canal was afterwards dug as I commanded, and ships passed from Egypt through this canal to Persia as was my will.

Darius's engineers may have been aware of the earlier waterway depicted in Queen Hatshepsut's temple. Some visible remains of the first Suez Canal must still have existed. Perhaps the engineers saved unnecessary labor and repaired the earlier canal whenever possible.

ANCIENT INDIA AND CHINA

Second century B.C. relief depicting scenes from the history of Buddhism; from a Buddhist shrine in Sanchi, Madhya Pradesh, India

The valleys of the region around the Indus River, between modern-day Pakistan and northern India, were the birthplace of Indian civilization. Farmers built settlements there that eventually became cities. They built dams and canals to control the flow of the river and to irrigate land farther away.

The Indus River Valley was fertile and produced more than enough grain and other crops to supply the population. The surplus could thus be traded for metals, timber, dye, and other products. Indus River Valley farmers were the first to grow cotton, and it too became a valuable item for trade. The Indians probably learned farming techniques from the Mesopotamians, who traded with them extensively.

Ancient Indian merchants exported fine cloth, jewels, pepper, and other spices along the famous Silk Road, a trade route that extended from China to the Mediterranean Sea. The Roman port of Ostia, 16 miles from Rome, had warehouses laden with pepper and other Indian

Indian gold coin minted around
A.D. 400 depicting an Indian
ruler, Chandragupta II

goods. The Indians traded only for gold. In fact, so much gold left Rome for India that the Roman emperor Nero, trying to prevent Rome from losing more gold, banned the import of peppercorns!

ROAD TRAVEL

The ancient Indians had an extensive system of roadways that impressed visitors from Greece and other nations. In fact, India even had the ancient equivalent of a Department of Transportation.

Rulers assigned an official in each region the job of over-seeing maintenance on the Royal Road, the main west-to-east route that linked the capital city of Pataliputra with the rest of the country. These transportation officials made sure that the road was free of obstructions and that markers were correctly positioned so that travelers could keep track of distances. The Royal Road was 1,700 miles long.

Regional governments helped merchants and other travelers by building rest houses along the Royal Road. These houses functioned much like modern motels. Travelers could get guidebooks describing the location of rest houses and other landmarks. There were even soldiers who served much like modern state troopers or highway patrols.

Emperor Asoka, who ruled from about 269 to 232 B.C., ordered that stone signs be erected along many roads in northern India. These huge pillars weighed up to 50 tons and were hauled to their roadside sites on oxcarts. The pillars were inscribed with Asoka's words of wisdom and advice for daily living. Proclaimed one: "It is good to give, but there is no gift, no service, like the gift of righteousness."

ELEPHANT POWER

For travel, trade, warfare, and construction work, the ancient Indians used the world's biggest and most powerful beast of burden—the elephant. The Indians recognized elephants as intelligent, easily trained animals. They captured young elephants in the wild and assigned each calf a keeper who stayed with it for life.

Elephants transported rulers and other wealthy people on saddles or in small covered compartments. They also carried packs of merchandise along trade routes. Elephants, the biggest of all land mammals, were ideal for logging in jungles. They could smash their way through heavy undergrowth while carrying logs with their powerful trunks.

Elephants are still used in some modern logging operations in India.

Elephants were also used in warfare. Soldiers rode on saddles fastened around the animals' necks and controlled the animals with voice commands and long sticks. In wartime, elephants even wore heavy leather armor for protection. Macedonian warrior Alexander the Great encountered these fighting animals when he and his army of 120,000 soldiers invaded India in 327 B.C.

THE BIG-TOE STIRRUP

Ancient Indians also fought on horseback. Indian riders introduced a major advance in warfare and transportation with the development of a simple device, the stirrup. A stirrup is a support that hangs down from each side of a saddle for the rider's foot. The device is so simple that some people might not even regard it as technology. Yet the stirrup was a revolutionary innovation.

Archaeologists have examined horses depicted in ancient statues, coins, and other artifacts. The artifacts show that most ancient groups did not use stirrups. Evidence suggests that Assyrian riders used stirrups as early as 835 B.C. But the first verified stirrups were introduced by ancient Indian riders between 300 B.C. and 200 B.C.

Stirrups made horses more accessible as a means of transportation. Just try mounting or dismounting a horse without using a stirrup. Without stirrups, riders had to vault onto horses, and only people in top physical condition could jump so high.

In warfare, stirrups transformed the horse into a battle platform. The saddle gave riders front and back balance, and stirrups added side-to-side balance. With stirrup and saddle, the horse and rider became a single stable unit. With weight on the stirrups, a rider could carry a long lance or spear, brace it firmly against the body, and charge an enemy. He could lift a heavy sword or battle ax high above his head and slash down hard without losing his balance.

The ancient Indian stirrup consisted of a fiber or leather thong attached to the saddle and draped against the horse's side. At the bottom was a loop, just big enough for the rider's big toe. Why the big toe rather than the entire foot? If you have the answer, archaeologists would love to know. In fact, the big-toe design may have slowed adoption of the stirrup by other groups. A stirrup of this kind could be used only in warm climates where people went barefoot.

Merchants and traders who traveled the Silk Road carried stirrup technology from India to China and eventually to Europe. Frankish King Charles Martel, who ruled the area that eventually became Germany and Belgium, adopted the stirrup in the eighth century A.D. Stirrups allowed Charles to develop a new, deadlier kind of warfare.

ANCIENT CHINA

Chinese civilization began between 5000 B.C. and 3000 B.C. in the Yellow River Valley of northern China. There, Stone Age people settled into small farming villages that grew into thriving cities. The river provided water for drinking, irrigation, fishing, and transportation. When the river flooded the land, it left behind layers of rich yellow soil that grew abundant crops.

China has many rivers, but few are connected to each other naturally. So the ancient Chinese developed technology to suit their geography. They dug numerous canals, changing their rivers into a watery transportation network that linked many parts of China.

Construction of the Grand Canal began around 600 B.C. It eventually extended more than six hundred miles through eastern China. Around 400 B.C., the Chinese dug the Wild Geese Canal to bring army troops from the Yellow

Modern junk in Hong Kong's harbor

River 250 miles south to the Huai River Valley. Shih Huang Ti, who became the first emperor of China in 221 B.C., ordered construction of the Magic Canal. Dug through a mountainous region, it made water transportation possible between northern and southern China.

THE MARVELOUS JUNK

To ply the canals, the ancient Chinese developed one of the ugliest and most awkward-looking ships of all time. Even its name, the *junk*, implies something inferior in our language. The name actually comes from a Portuguese word, *junco*, which is a plant used in rigging.

Junks were unattractive. With a flat bottom, high stern (rear), and low bow (front), they looked boxy and ungainly. Junks lacked three components that most people regarded as fundamental to ships. They had no keel (a long beam along the bottom of a boat that keeps it together), no stemposts, and no sternpost (upright members at bow and stern, respectively). Yet junks were among the strongest and most seaworthy vessels ever designed.

The high stern, for instance, allowed the deck to stay dry when waves crashed from behind. The design also assured that the ship would safely turn with its bow to the wind when anchored. A flat bottom allowed safe sailing through shallow water and easy beaching to unload cargo.

A rudder, or heavy steering oar, compensated for the lack of a keel. The rudder was mounted in a watertight shaft, extending through the deck and hull. The rudder could be raised in shallow water to prevent damage and lowered again with ease.

Sails were made of bamboo mats or linen fabric. They

were secured in a way that allowed crew members to open and close them quickly with changing wind conditions.

A major advantage of the boxy design was an exceptionally strong hull, or main body of a boat. Bulkheads—solid walls made from heavy wooden planks—ran lengthwise and crosswise inside the hull and divided it into 12 or more watertight compartments. The compartments limited damage if the ship struck rock or was damaged in battle. A hole in the hull might flood one compartment, but it probably would not sink the entire ship.

Bulkheads were a truly revolutionary advance in shipbuilding. In Marco Polo's *Travels*, written in A.D. 1298, the Italian traveler praised the bulkhead system's stability in the event that the ship "springs a leak by running against a rock, or on being hit by a hungry whale." Yet bulkheads were not adopted by the West until the nineteenth century A.D. Junks are still used in China, but often with small motors to provide auxiliary power.

THE WOODEN OX

For land transport, the ancient Chinese had a simple yet ingenious device that enabled a single person to move heavy loads. The device consisted of a wooden frame with a wheel and two handles for lifting and pushing. The Chinese called the vehicle the Gliding Horse or the Wooden Ox. We call it the wheelbarrow.

A Chinese general, Jugo Liang, usually gets credit for inventing the wheelbarrow around A.D. 230, though recently discovered paintings from ancient tombs suggest that someone else may have invented the wheelbarrow around A.D. 100. Liang wanted an inexpensive, simple, easy-to-maintain vehicle that would help his soldiers transport huge quantities of food, weapons, and other equipment.

With the wheelbarrow, one man could carry a load that had previously required two or three people. One military porter with a wheelbarrow could carry enough food to supply four soldiers for three months. The first Chinese wheelbarrows had the wheel in the middle—directly under the load. With this arrangement, the pusher's main work involved balancing and steering. (Modern wheelbarrows, with the wheel at one end, require people to use much more effort to lift and support the load.)

The Chinese used wheelbarrows to transport people and goods such as rice and vegetables. Some later versions of wheelbarrows could hold several passengers.

Europeans didn't make use of this simple transportation aid for almost a thousand years. It wasn't until the twelfth century A.D. that workers building great cathedrals in Europe began using wheelbarrows to haul heavy loads.

THE SILK ROAD

During the Han dynasty, from 202 B.C. to A.D. 220, Chinese merchants drove caravans of camels from cities along

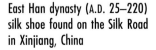

East Han dynasty (A.D. 25–220) silk shoe found on the Silk Road in Xinjiang, China

the Yellow River through central Asia to the Middle East. These merchants traded jade, lacquerware, and bronze for rugs, horses, glass, and other products. But the main Chinese export was silk, which then was produced only in China by a secret process. So much silk traveled over this route that it became known as the Silk Road, the most famous trade route in the ancient world.

Few merchants made the entire trip, which extended thousands of miles overland from Ch'ang-an in east central China through modern Siberia, to the eastern coast of the Mediterranean, and then by sea to Rome and Venice. Rather, goods changed hands many times along the road.

The Silk Road became an ancient technological superhighway. Merchants exchanged information about new ideas and technology. For instance, the tandem hitching of horses (one behind the other) saved space on narrow roads. The Chinese began this practice and passed it on to the Western world. Thanks to trading on the Silk Road, everybody benefited from this new technology.

A Spoon Points the Way

In *The Book of the Devil Valley Master,* written in the fourth century B.C., philosopher Su Ch'in states: "When the people of Cheng go out to collect jade, they carry a south-pointer with them, so as not to lose their way." Another ancient Chinese writer remarks, "When the south-controlling spoon is thrown upon the ground, it comes to rest pointing to the south." The "south-pointer" or "magic spoon" the ancient writers refer to is the magnetic compass, and it was in practical use in China by the fourth century B.C.

Mariners, hikers, aviators, and other travelers frequently

Chinese *sinan,* or compass, made around 2,300 years ago

use magnetic compasses for navigation. Compasses indicate direction with a needle that points to the earth's north magnetic pole. With north established, people can determine other directions, including their direction of travel, from the compass's face.

The ancient Chinese used a compass called a *sinan.* It was made of lodestone, a magnetic form of iron, fashioned into the shape of a ladle. When placed on a polished slab of stone, the spoon moved in the earth's magnetic field. The bowl of the spoon pointed north, and the handle pointed south. Marks indicating direction—north, south, east, and west—were carved on the slab's surface.

Can you guess why the Chinese chose a ladle for the

shape of their compass? Here's a clue: *dipper* is another word for a ladle. The ladle shape represented the Big Dipper, a constellation whose stars align with the North Star. When mariners navigate "by the stars," they often use the Big Dipper as a pointer.

Arab traders learned about the compass from the Chinese and told Europeans about it in the fourteenth century A.D. This basic tool of navigation helped make possible such great sea voyages as Christopher Columbus's voyages to the New World, during what came to be known as the "Age of Exploration."

Modern ships and aircraft use a gyrocompass, a more accurate device introduced in the twentieth century A.D. It consists of a wheel spinning on an axis aligned with earth's own axis of rotation.

ANCIENT MESOAMERICA

Mayan temple at Chichén Itzá, Mexico

About 30,000 years ago, present-day Siberia and Alaska were connected by a land bridge called Beringia. Using this bridge, Stone Age people from Asia were able to cross into North America. (Beringia surfaced when sea levels fell during the last ice age. When the earth warmed and sea levels rose about 10,000 years ago, Beringia was again covered by water.) Other Asian peoples may have reached North America by walking over thick ice in the Bering Strait between Siberia and Alaska. Still others may have reached the Americas by boat over open stretches of ocean.

Like other Stone Age people, the first North Americans were hunters and gatherers. They probably crossed Beringia to follow herds of bison, mastodons, and mammoths that migrated to Alaska. People then moved south through present-day Canada, onto the American Great Plains, and into present-day Mexico and Central America. These Paleo-Indians (ancient Indians) reached the tip of South America by about

11,000 B.C. Different groups encountered different environmental conditions as they migrated south, and separate cultures developed throughout the Americas.

We have few artifacts and no written records of the Paleo-Indians' transportation technology. Archaeologists assume that hunter-gatherers in North America relied on foot coverings, yokes, travois, and other technology like that used by hunter-gatherers in the Old World.

CITIES AND PALACES

Great civilizations emerged in Mesoamerica, which extended from Mexico to the Isthmus of Panama in Central America. The Olmec civilization began on the eastern coast of Mexico before 1200 B.C. and declined around 100 B.C. Among the Olmecs' best-known achievements were huge carved stone heads. Some of them were nine feet tall and weighed 20 tons!

The Maya emerged around 2500 B.C. and developed a great empire in what are now southern Mexico, Guatemala, Belize, El Salvador, and Honduras. Many aspects of Mayan civilization rivaled or surpassed those of Old World civilizations such as Egypt and Greece. The Maya developed advanced farming and irrigation methods. They built cities with paved streets. They used huge stone blocks to build temple-pyramids and palaces. They developed a written language and made accurate astronomical observations. Mayan mathematicians understood the concept of zero, an idea that eluded the best mathematicians in ancient Greece and Rome. The civilization reached a peak between A.D. 300 and A.D. 700, then mysteriously declined.

There are few written records from the Mesoamerican

civilizations. Much of what we know about Mesoamerican transportation technology actually comes from the Spanish, who arrived in A.D. 1519, thousands of years after the end of ancient times.

LEARNING MORE

Archaeologists have studied artifacts and ruins of ancient cities to learn more about Mesoamerican civilizations. They have found the remains of Mayan ports, including one on the island of Cerritos off the northern coast of the Yucatán Peninsula. The port facilities, used between 300 B.C. and A.D. 300, included piers, docks, and an artificial canal. A seawall, more than a thousand feet long, protected boats in the harbor. Mayan merchants probably brought canoes full of salt, fish, and other goods to the port for trading.

Archaeologists have also learned that the Maya traded between lowland and highland regions. Products from the

Giant Olmec stone head from Villahermosa, Mexico, carved around 1500 B.C.

tropical lowlands—salt, cacao (chocolate), cotton, feathers, spices, jaguar pelts, and other goods—have been found in the remains of ancient settlements throughout the highlands. Highland products such as jade and obsidian (a volcanic glass used to make knife blades and other tools) have been found in the lowlands.

QUESTIONS REMAIN

How did the Olmec move colossal stone blocks? How did the Maya transport huge amounts of food from farms to feed large urban populations? What vehicles did they use?

Archaeologists know that the Maya used boats to travel by water. Perhaps the Olmec moved stone blocks on sledges, as did other ancient peoples. If so, the sledges were probably pulled by people—because the Mesoamericans never harnessed beasts of burden. Nor did they ever use the wheel for transportation.

Why not? The Mesoamerican groups had plenty of wood that could have been used to make wheels. But their terrain was not suitable for wheeled vehicles. Many Mesoamerican settlements were located in rugged upland regions and in tropical rain forests. Without land that was relatively flat, dry, and firm, wheeled vehicles were not useful.

The Mesoamericans lacked another requirement for wheeled transportation. They had no draft animals to pull vehicles. The Maya may have domesticated deer to use for food. But they did not use them as draft animals. Ironically, archaeologists have found wheels in ancient Mayan ruins. But these were used only on children's toys.

ANCIENT GREECE

Detail of a vase painting from 540 B.C. depicting Greek god Dionysus in his boat

Greece, **birthplace of great** ancient philosophers, writers, and artists, is a rugged land. Ancient Greek farmers grew grapes, olives, and other fruits. But their farms were small, and the Greeks had to look beyond their borders for a greater supply of food. Almost everywhere they looked, they saw ocean.

It's no wonder, then, that the ancient Greeks excelled at shipbuilding, mapmaking, seafaring, trading, and naval warfare. Geography often plays a role in the development of technology, and the ancient Greeks' most important contributions to transportation technology involved the sea.

In 338 B.C., Philip of Macedonia conquered the Greek city-states and established Greece as a military power. Philip's son, Alexander the Great, then conquered much of the Mediterranean and Near Eastern world—from Egypt to India. Greece's strength stemmed in large part from its superior seafaring technology.

BEACONS FOR MARINERS

Lighthouses are beacons that guide mariners into harbors or warn of rocky shorelines that could sink a ship. A Greek poet named Lesches, who lived around 660 B.C., described what historians regard as the first regularly maintained lighthouse. It was located near the village of Sigeum on the coast of northwestern Turkey.

The ancient Greeks anchored their fleet of warships at Sigeum during a 10-year war with Troy. The Sigeum light guarded the entrance to a strait called the Dardanelles. This narrow channel provides an opening for ships to pass between the Mediterranean and Black Seas. By ruling the strait, the Greeks could thus control oceangoing trade and travel in a huge region of the world.

WONDROUS LIGHTHOUSE

The most famous ancient lighthouse was the Pharos of Alexandria, built on a rocky island off the northern coast of Egypt in the Mediterranean Sea. The Pharos faced the great ancient city of Alexandria, from which the Greeks ruled Egypt.

Ptolemy II, who ruled Egypt from 283 to 246 B.C., ordered the construction of the lighthouse. It was an important part of his plan to revitalize Egypt's economy by increasing trade with other countries. The light guided cargo-laden merchant ships through the harbor of Alexandria. It also served as an enormous symbol of Ptolemy's power and Egypt's revival. Indeed, the Pharos of Alexandria was regarded as one of the Seven Wonders of the Ancient World.

An earthquake destroyed the lighthouse in the fourteenth

century A.D., so we have little accurate information about its construction. But it must have been magnificent. Some accounts indicate that the Pharos towered to a height of six hundred feet—as high as a 60-story skyscraper. Others put the height at 350 feet. It was built of stone, with a square base, an octagonal (eight-sided) midsection, and a round upper tower. A light in the tower burned so brightly that sailors could see it 30 miles away. What did the lighthouse tenders burn? Probably wood, but nobody knows for sure.

The light became so famous that *pharos* came to mean "lighthouse" in Greek and many other languages. The word is *faro* in Italian and *phare* in French. People who study lighthouse construction are even called pharologists.

Another of the Seven Wonders of the Ancient World, the Colossus of Rhodes, was also a lighthouse. It was located on Rhodes, an island in the southwestern Aegean Sea. Rhodes was an independent kingdom and a center for trade and commerce until its destruction by an earthquake in 155 B.C. The Colossus was built around 280 B.C. at the entrance to the Rhodes harbor.

The Colossus was both a lighthouse and a monument to the sun god Helios, to whom Rhodians prayed for deliverance during war. We know little about the lighthouse itself. But the monument was the ancient world's equivalent of the Statue of Liberty. One drawing depicts the Colossus as a nude man standing on a pedestal, gazing eastward over the sea. He wears a spiky crown of solar rays on his head. A cloak is draped over one arm, and the other is raised to shield his eyes from the rising sun.

An earthquake turned the Colossus into a colossal junk

heap in 224 B.C., so we have little reliable information about its construction. Some medieval stories, written a thousand years after its destruction, claim the Colossus was 900 feet high. Ancient writers, however, described the Colossus as 70 cubits high. There are different definitions of a cubit, and that has led to confusion about the exact size of the Colossus. But it was probably between 90 to 120 feet high. The Statue of Liberty, in comparison, rises 111 feet when measured from foot to crown.

TRIREMES

The standard battleship in ancient Greece was the trireme, a swift galley (a boat powered by rowers) and equipped with a heavy battering ram on the front for sinking enemy ships. A typical trireme was about 140 feet long and 10 feet wide.

The word *trireme* comes from the Latin *triremis*, which means "having three oars to each bench." The vessels were outfitted with three banks, or decks, of rowers. The top bank had 31 men, with 27 in each lower bank. With each man pulling a single oar, the outside of a trireme looked like a porcupine.

Triremes evolved from the Phoenician bireme, an earlier, smaller vessel which had two decks of rowers. Triremes eventually evolved into bigger and more awesome fighting ships. The last of these were giants propelled by thousands of rowers, with up to 16 men pulling each huge oar.

ANCIENT FREIGHTERS

Alexandria was an important ancient trade center. Hundreds of merchant ships sailed trade routes to and from the

Modern full-size replica of the trireme *Olympia*

city at the mouth of the Nile. The ships were laden with wine, olive oil, corn, wheat, fruit, timber, fabrics, dyes, hides, live animals, and a tremendous assortment of other goods.

Shipping costs were determined by the same factors 2,300 years ago as they are in modern times. A key factor was the amount of cargo on a ship. Big ships transporting lots of cargo could operate for less money. The ancient Greeks thus built big cargo ships. Most could hold 150 tons of freight. The standard Greek grain ship carried 340 tons. Some ships carried even more. By contrast, caravels, the most advanced ships built in fifteenth century A.D.

Spain and Portugal (Christopher Columbus's *Niña* and *Pinta* were caravels) held only about 125 tons.

AND SUPER-FREIGHTERS

No ancient cargo ship could match the *Syracusa*, a monster built around 250 B.C. for King Hiero II of Syracuse. It had three masts hung with acres of sail and 20 banks of rowers. It carried around two thousand tons. No one would build a ship that even approached the *Syracusa's* capacity for almost two thousand more years.

Like many other trading vessels, the *Syracusa* was heavily armed for protection against pirates. It had armored turrets equipped with catapults and a supply of large rocks for ammunition. The ship carried a guard of two hundred marines.

We don't know the ship's dimensions, the size of its crew, or the number of passengers it could carry. But it certainly was lavishly equipped. It carried 20,000 gallons of freshwater and wooden tanks of seawater filled with live fish. It had a stable for horses, a kitchen with stoves and ovens, storerooms for food and other provisions, and even a library and a gymnasium.

How fast could a super-freighter sail? Greek ships were built not for speed but to carry a lot of cargo and to withstand pirates and storms. Even with favorable winds billowing their sails, most Greek freighters could travel at only about six knots—about seven miles per hour.

"WHAT A MONSTER SHE WAS!"

The arrival of Greek ships into port created great excitement, and whole cities turned out to admire them. The

Greek writer Lucian, who lived from A.D. 120 to 180, described the stir at one port at the arrival of *Isis*, a 1,228-ton freighter:

> What a monster she was! All of 180 feet in length, so the ship's carpenter told me . . . and a full 44 feet from the deck to the bottom of her hold. And the height of the mast! The whole ship was a dream! She had a crew as big as an army, and enough grain aboard to feed the whole of Athens for a year!

BOAT BRIDGES

Some experts believe that boat bridges—chains of boats tied together to span rivers—were the first long bridges. Armies often used boat bridges because they could be built quickly. The Greek historian Herodotus, who traveled over most of the known world of his time, wrote several accounts of these bridges. One comes from his account of the wars between Greece and Persia in the fifth century B.C.:

> They laid 50 oared ships and triremes alongside of each other. . . . Having so laid the ships alongside they let down very great anchors, both from the end of the ship nearest the Pontus to hold fast against the winds blowing from within that sea. . . . Moreover, they left for passage an opening in the line of 50 oared ships and triremes . . . they stretched the cables from the land, twisting them taut with wooden windlasses. . . . When the strait was thus bridged, they sawed balks of wood to a length equal to the breadth of the floating supports, and laid them in order on taut cables. . . . This done they heaped brushwood on to the bridge, and when this was laid in order they heaped earth on it and stamped it down, then they made a fence on either side, lest the beasts of burden and horses should be affrighted by the sight of the sea below them.

THE FIRST MARATHON

The Greeks didn't do all their travel by sea, however. On land, running was actually one of the fastest ways of transporting messages. Kings, government officials, and generals used runners just like modern businesspeople use overnight mail and package delivery services.

The most famous message ever delivered by foot was sent during the Persian Wars in 490 B.C. A Persian army landed at Marathon, about 25 miles north of Athens, and was defeated by a smaller Greek force. The Greeks wanted to get news of the victory to Athens as quickly as possible. According to legend, they turned to their fastest runner, who had just returned from a 150-mile trip to Sparta. Nonetheless, he took the assignment, reached Athens, cried

Bronze figurine of a girl running, made in the sixth century B.C.

out, "Rejoice, we are victorious," and dropped dead. The modern marathon, 26 miles, 385 yards, is named in honor of this run.

THE FATHER OF EQUITATION

Horses were as essential for transportation in the ancient world as automobiles are in modern times. They also were critical weapons, whose performance often meant the difference between life and death in battle. Ancient people thus were eager for advice on the proper care and handling of these valuable pieces of living technology.

A Greek cavalryman named Xenophon, who lived from 430 to 335 B.C., wrote the world's first fully preserved manual on the training and care of horses. It was entitled *The Art of Horsemanship*. Much of Xenophon's advice remains the best available, even after almost 2,500 years. He observed, for instance:

> The one great precept and practice in using a horse is this—never deal with him when you are in a fit of passion. When your horse shies at an object and is unwilling to go up to it, he should be shown there is nothing fearful in it, least of all to a courageous horse like him. But if this fails, touch the object yourself that seems so dreadful to him, and lead him up to it with gentleness. Compulsion and blows inspire only the more fear; and when horses are at all hurt at such times, they think what they shied at is the cause of the hurt.

EARTH IS ROUND!

The Babylonians were great mapmakers who introduced such key elements as cardinal points (north, south, east, west) and scales that related distance on a map to actual distances on earth. From that base of knowledge, the Greeks made several technological leaps in mapping.

Historians believe that Greek scholars were the first to realize that the earth is round rather than flat. Some trace the idea of a round earth to Pythagoras, a mathematician who lived from 580 to 500 B.C. Others think the idea originated with Parmenides, who was born around 515 B.C. In approximately 350 B.C., the Greek philosopher Aristotle developed six arguments for a round earth that convinced most scholars. Contrary to popular belief, scholars agreed that the earth was round long before Christopher Columbus's first voyage in A.D. 1492.

BASICS OF NAVIGATION

One of the foundations of navigation at sea is figuring out the position and course of a ship. Position is a specific point on the earth's surface. Finding it requires a set of coordinates. Latitude and longitude are the key.

Latitude is distance north or south of the equator, measured in degrees. Each degree of latitude is about 69 miles. Longitude is distance east or west of the prime meridian, a line running from the North Pole to the South Pole through Greenwich, England. At the equator, each degree of longitude also equals 69 miles.

The revolutionary concept of using latitude and longitude to identify points on a map originated around 300 B.C. Working with a map of the world, a Greek scholar named Dicaearchus drew a latitude line that extended east and west through Rhodes and Gibraltar. Others scholars later extended the point-of-reference concept to include lines of longitude.

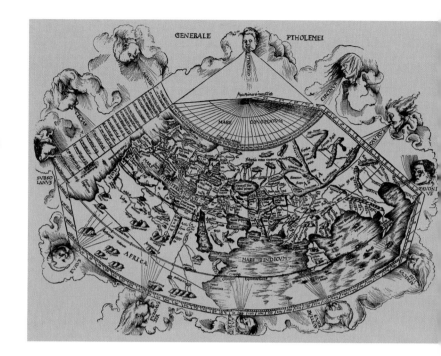

Ptolemy's map of the world, drawn in the second century A.D.

BETTER MAPMAKERS

Many ancient maps were based on stories from travelers and soldiers. Few mapmakers actually traveled, saw land features firsthand, or made their own diagrams and notes.

Herodotus was an exception. He visited many countries and accurately recorded geographic details. When he compared his own personal knowledge with the maps he saw, Herodotus had one response:

> It makes me laugh when I see some people drawing maps of the world without having any reason to guide them; they show the Ocean running like a river round the earth, and the earth itself to be an exact circle, as if drawn by a pair of compasses, with Europe and Asia just of the same size.

Herodotus drew his own map of the world, depicting countries, bodies of water, cities, and other geographical features in a more accurate perspective.

One of the greatest innovators in mapmaking was Ptolemy, an astronomer and scholar who lived in the second century A.D. He wrote an encyclopedic, eight-volume treatise on geography. It included the most accurate map of the world to that point in history. The map identified more than eight thousand places and listed their latitude and longitude.

Ptolemy's map was the basis for all world maps produced in Europe for the next 1,300 years. When Ptolemy's *Geography* was translated into Latin in A.D. 1406, it helped people realize the extent and nature of the world. The maps that Christopher Columbus used on his first voyage across the Atlantic were based on Ptolemy's map.

Of course, Ptolemy's map contained errors. It underestimated the size of the earth and showed Europe and Asia as spanning half the globe. Columbus, sailing west in an effort to circle the globe, thus underestimated the length of the voyage to his intended landing point, India. Would Columbus have been daring enough to set out on the voyage if he had known the truth?

ANCIENT ROME

First century B.C. relief of a Roman
mail coach

Many modern advances in technology, especially in transportation, result from military research and development programs. Governments spend billions of dollars each year to develop new aircraft and weapons. Some people criticize this as a dangerous waste of money. Others note that such work can lead to new technology that benefits society.

In the ancient world, Rome was a great military power. The Romans conquered many other countries and developed an empire that stretched through much of Europe, the Mediterranean region, and the Near East.

Rome took part in its own arms race. Its military needed a fast, reliable way of transporting armies, supplies, and messages to distant parts of the empire. To fill that need, Rome built the ancient world's greatest highway system.

WOODEN ROADS

The first paved roads in Rome were made from wood. Wedge-shaped foundation boards were cut from oak or alder trees and placed angled side down for greater stability. Paving boards were laid on top and fastened with wooden stakes. Engineers overlapped the paving boards, so that the thick edge of one covered the thin edge of the next.

Other wooden roads, sometimes built over soft or swampy ground, were elevated. Stakes, sometimes seven feet long, were pounded into the soil. The ends rose above the surface to a uniform elevation. The tops of the stakes were then covered with boards. A layer of gravel served as pavement.

These wooden roads proved to be remarkably durable. Sections of the roads, some of which are 13 feet wide, can still be found in parts of Europe.

ROADS BUILT TO LAST

The most durable Roman roads were made of layers of packed earth, stone blocks, sand, and other materials. Some roads were five feet thick. They were paved with blocks of cut stone or rocks mixed with mortar.

Roads through rainy areas had a cambered, or arched, surface—higher in the center than at the sides. This shape made water drain off the surface, so it would not soak into the road and damage it. (Modern roads still use this same cambered design.) Most roads had curbstones and drainage ditches at the sides. Stretches of road through towns had elevated sidewalks, so pedestrians could walk safely.

Many ancient civilizations, including the Mesopotamians, Egyptians, Indians, Chinese, and Greeks, built paved roads for the military. But none matched the system of roads begun in 312 B.C. by the Roman ruler Claudius Appius.

Remains of a Roman road in Sicily, Italy

His system included more than 370 major roads that extended about 50,000 miles and connected all the large towns of the Roman territories—from Greece to Spain to Scotland. Markers placed every thousand paces (about 1,620 yards) along the roads told troops how far they had traveled.

The oldest and most famous road was the Via Appia, or Appian Way, which went southward from the Servian Wall in Rome to Capua. The road was more than 350 miles long and 35 feet wide. Like many other Roman roads, the Appian Way was built as straight as possible.

Why were the roads so straight? Because a straight line is the shortest distance between two towns? No, because Roman wagons had fixed axles that could not be moved to steer the vehicle. Wagons could only travel straight, so roads had to follow. To get a wagon off a road, workers had to inch it to the curb with huge pry bars.

ROAD SERVICE

The Roman government had an official courier service, the *cursus publicus*, that delivered mail throughout the territories. Couriers traveled on horseback as fast as possible. When horses became exhausted, couriers could get new ones at posts along the roads. There were posts every 10 miles. They had large stables of horses and attendants, including veterinarians.

There were also roadhouses where travelers could buy a meal, sleep, and rest their horses. *Mansiones* were elaborate roadhouses for government officials. Public roadhouses served more ordinary travelers, but they were dangerous places where guests were sometimes robbed. Many travelers preferred to stay with friends or relatives instead.

ANCIENT TRIP-TIKS

No, the American Automobile Association did not invent Trip-Tiks, packets of maps and directions used by many modern travelers. Ancient Roman travelers used similar guides, called *itineraria* (after the Latin word *itinerari*, meaning "to travel").

Itineraria were written on parchment or papyrus and were used by soldiers, merchants, farmers, pilgrims, and civil servants traveling on government business. The guides showed the location of famous tombs and other sight-seeing attractions, as well as roadhouses, bridges, rivers, and other features along roads. Trip-Tiks often mention road hazards or areas of construction. Itineraria did the same, but focused on problems of greater concern to ancient travelers—such as hungry wolves in an area.

Experts believe that the master source for many itineraria may have been the Peutinger Table. This parchment scroll showed all the roads of the Roman Empire, from India to Britain, and some nearby countries. The table showed the location of roadhouses and bathhouses. It showed distances and the most efficient routes between towns. Information was presented in five colors. The Peutinger Table probably was based on a map of the world drawn by Marcus Agrippa, a Roman general who lived from 63 to 12 B.C.

Unfortunately, few original ancient maps survived Europe's early Middle Ages, the period from A.D. 476 to about A.D. 1000, when few people cared about learning and knowledge. Progress in mapping and other fields of science and technology stopped. We have only copies of most ancient maps. Many of these are copies of copies. We don't know how accurately scholars followed the originals. Maybe each scholar added personal artistic touches.

ANCIENT TRAFFIC LAWS

Even in ancient times, there were traffic jams, especially in the city of Rome. There were periods of gridlock, when ox carts, chariots, handcarts, mounted horses, and farm wagons could barely move. The Roman senate enacted traffic laws—setting up stop signs, one-way streets, and parking places. But traffic was still unbearable in Rome. Finally, ruler Julius Caesar, who lived from about 100 to 44 B.C., enacted the Lex Iulia Municipalis, an urban law that banned certain vehicles from city streets in the daytime.

WARSHIPS

Rome did not dominate just on land. Rome controlled the Mediterranean Sea for centuries and built many warships to maintain its power. Some ships had catapults for hurling stones at enemies and pirates. Some ships had movable bridges that allowed soldiers to board enemy vessels.

The *dromon* was the ultimate Roman warship. It was used in the Roman Empire after the fourth century A.D. This swift vessel had sails, banks of rowers, and high-tech armor made from leather and cloth. The armor was soaked with vinegar and other fluids, which kept ships from catching on fire when hit by hot stones or flaming arrows.

ANCIENT LIFE PRESERVERS

Remember the inflated sheepskins that people in Mesopotamia used as water floats? These floats worked well, but had a big disadvantage. Even with the most skillful construction, they constantly lost air from their seams and frequently had to be reinflated.

The ancient Romans introduced a "swimming belt" that improved on Mesopotamian float technology. The belt was a leather tube filled with cork, a material that is buoyant and floats. A poor swimmer, or a person unable to swim at all, could use the swimming belt to cross a river or survive a shipwreck. The first record of a Roman swimming belt dates to 390 B.C. It describes a military messenger who used a swimming belt to reach Rome by crossing the Tiber River.

PORTS

In some ways, ports were even more important in the ancient world than in modern times. Most trade and communication involved rivers and oceans in ancient times, and ports were the places where water travel began and ended. Ports also were places where people of diverse backgrounds met and exchanged ideas, culture, and technology.

One important ancient port was Cosa, located north of Rome on the Mediterranean coast. At its peak, around 100 B.C., Cosa made, packaged, and shipped two main products: dried, salted fish and wine. Both items were staples of the Roman diet.

Cosa had its own fish farming operation, with a huge natural lagoon and about 2.5 acres of concrete fish tanks. According to archaeologists, the tanks alone could have yielded 3.3 million pounds of fish each year.

There were facilities for salting and drying fish and for processing the most famous and expensive condiment in ancient Rome: garum. Garum was made from salted fish guts that were fermented in the sun. People used it like ketchup. A bottle of garum cost 10 times more than a bottle of the best wine.

Fish processing required large amounts of freshwater, and Cosa had an elaborate pumping station, powered by slaves and criminals. Wine was made at a winery near the harbor, with local farmers supplying grapes in ox-drawn carts.

Port facilities were well designed. A breakwater, a wall of limestone blocks, protected vessels from incoming waves and prevented silt from filling in the harbor. Two piers for loading and unloading ships were built on the breakwater, and three more were nearby on concrete piles. Evidence suggests that Cosa had a lighthouse that was more than 90 feet high.

SHIPPING CONTAINERS

Wine and olive oil were among the most important products in ancient times. These valuable liquids had to be stored in watertight containers. The containers themselves had to be easy to load onto ships.

Relief of a merchant offering amphorae (shipping containers) to the gods

The main shipping container in the ancient world was the amphora, a pottery jug with two handles. The typical amphora was three feet tall and had a capacity of 26 quarts.

The industrial complex at Cosa had its own amphora factory. Using mass production techniques, the factory made tens of thousands of amphorae annually.

2,300 YEARS LATER

Ancient times ended and the Middle Ages began with the collapse of the Western Roman Empire in A.D. 476. Roman roads began to deteriorate because of a lack of maintenance. Even so, they remained the best roads in Europe for centuries. Not a single new highway was built in Europe for more than five hundred years after Rome fell. Can you believe that parts of the Appian Way are still in use? They carry car and truck traffic after more than 2,300 years.

GLOSSARY

artifact—an object made by people, such as a tool or ornament, especially an object remaining from a certain period in time

cardinal points—the four principal compass points: north, south, east, and west

compass—a device with a magnetic needle that is used to determine direction

domesticate—to adapt an animal or plant for human use

latitude—a measurement of distance north or south of the earth's equator

longitude—a measurement of distance east or west of the earth's prime meridian

Seven Wonders of the Ancient World—a listing of the world's greatest engineering feats drawn up by ancient Greek writers

sledge—a flat vehicle such as a sleigh, used to drag objects across the ground; powered by people or animals

travois—a vehicle consisting of two poles and sometimes an attached sled, dragged by a person or animal across the ground

yoke—a pole carried across the shoulder, used to transport items

BIBLIOGRAPHY

Aust, Siegfried. *Ships! Come Aboard.* Minneapolis: Lerner Publications, 1993.

Bunch, Bryan H., and Alexander Hellemans. *The Timetables of Technology: A Chronology of the Most Important People and Events in the History of Technology.* New York: Simon & Schuster, 1993.

Cotterell, Arthur. *China's Civilization: A Survey of Its History, Arts and Technology.* New York: Praeger, 1975.

De Bono, Edward. *Eureka! How and When the Greatest Inventions Were Made.* New York: Holt, Rinehart, and Winston, 1974.

Dilke, O. A. W. *The Ancient Romans: How They Lived and Worked.* Chester Springs, Pa.: Dufour Editions, 1975.

Humble, Richard. *Ships: Sailors and the Sea.* New York: Franklin Watts, 1991.

James, Peter, and Nick Thorpe. *Ancient Inventions.* New York: Ballantine, 1994.

Johnstone, Paul. *The Seacraft of Prehistory.* Cambridge, Mass.: Harvard University Press, 1980.

Kerrod, Robin. T*ransportation: From the Bicycle to Spacecraft.* New York: Macmillan, 1991.

"Legacy of the Horse." *The International Museum of the Horse.* <http://www.imh.org> (8 December 1998).

Neuberger, Albert. *The Technical Arts and Sciences of the Ancients.* New York: Barnes & Noble, 1969.

Perry, Marvin. *A History of the Ancient World.* Boston: Houghton Mifflin, 1985.

Saggs, H. W. F. *Civilization Before Greece and Rome.* New Haven: Yale University Press, 1989.

Starr, Chester G., Jr., ed. *A History of the Ancient World.* New York: Oxford University Press, 1991.

White, K. D. *Greek and Roman Technology.* Ithaca, NY: Cornell University Press, 1984.

Wilkinson, Philip, ed. *Early Humans.* New York: Knopf, 1989.

INDEX

Note: There are alternate spellings for some of the names mentioned in this book. Here are a few examples:
Ramses or Ramesses or Rameses (Egypt)
Khufu or Cheops (Egypt)
Asoka or Ashoka (India)
Shih Huang Ti or Shi Huang Di (China)
Herodotus or Herodotos (Greece)

About the Authors

Michael Woods is an award-winning science and medical writer with the Washington bureau of the *Toledo Blade* and the *Pittsburgh Post Gazette*. His articles and weekly health column, "The Medical Journal," appear in newspapers around the United States. Born in Dunkirk, New York, Mr. Woods developed a love for science and writing in childhood and studied both topics in school. His many awards include an honorary doctorate degree for helping to develop the profession of science writing. His previous work includes a children's book on Antarctica, where he has traveled on three expeditions.

Mary B. Woods is an elementary school librarian in the Fairfax County, Virginia, public school system. Born in New Rochelle, New York, Mrs. Woods studied history in college and later received a master's degree in library science. She is coauthor of a children's book on new discoveries about the ancient Maya civilization.

Photo Acknowledgments: E.T. Archive: (Musee Royale d'art, Brussels) p. 1, (Anthropological Institute Turin) p. 11, (E.T. Archive) p. 85; © Christopher Liu/ChinaStock, pp. 2–3, 47, 57, 59; Art Resource: (Werner Forman Archive) pp. 12–13, (British Museum, London/Werner Forman Archive) p. 23, (© Erich Lessing) pp. 37, 45, 68–69, 82–83; Karlene Schwartz, p. 15; Corbis: (Gianni Dagli Orti) p. 19, (Bob Rowan, Progressive Image) p. 54; The Granger Collection, pp. 20, 29; Ancient Art & Architecture Collection, Ltd: (© Ronald Sheridan) pp. 24–25, 30–31, 50, 90, (© Stephen Gore) p. 65, (© Mike Andrews) p. 73; Kenneth Garrett, pp. 34, 38–39; © Richard Nowitz, p. 41; Bridgeman Art Library, London/New York: (British Museum, London/Ancient Art & Architecture Collection, Ltd.) p. 42, (British Museum, London) p. 76; © Ilay Cooper/Images of India, pp. 48–49; © Max & Bea Hunn/DDB Stock Photography, p. 61; © Gary Braasch, pp. 62–63; AKG London: p. 67, (Gilles Mermet) p. 81; Library of Congress, p. 79.

Front cover photographs courtesy of: Grant Smith/Corbis (left), Archaeological Museum Cairo/E.T. Archive (right)